READERS THEATRE
FOR
BEGINNING READERS

READERS THEATRE
FOR
BEGINNING READERS

SUZANNE I. BARCHERS

TEACHER IDEAS PRESS
A Division of
Libraries Unlimited, Inc.
Englewood, Colorado
1993

Dedicated to
Charla Pfeffinger
and
Connie Mantarro

TEACHER IDEAS PRESS
A Division of Libraries Unlimited, Inc.
P.O. Box 6633
Englewood, CO 80155-6633
1-800-237-6124

Library of Congress Cataloging-in-Publication Data

Barchers, Suzanne I.
      Readers theatre for beginning readers / Suzanne I. Barchers.
      vii, 97 p. 22x28 cm.
      Includes bibliographical references and index.
      ISBN 1-56308-136-9
      1. Children's plays, American. 2. Readers' theater. I. Title.
PS3552.A5988R4   1993
812'.54--dc20   92-45813
                                                                   CIP

CONTENTS

PART 3

ACKNOWLEDGMENTS

Grateful appreciation is extended to Susan Carlson and her second-graders and Linda Gouin and her first-graders for their willingness to test and critique this book. Their suggestions were invaluable.

Grateful acknowledgment is made for permission to adapt "The Half Chick" from *The Green Fairy Book*, edited by Andrew Lang, Dover Publications, 1965. "Kumba and Kambili" was adapted from *Wise Women: Folk and Fairy Tales from Around the World* by Suzanne I. Barchers, Libraries Unlimited, 1990.

INTRODUCTION

THE ROLE OF READERS THEATRE

"Readers theatre is a presentation by two or more participants who read from scripts and interpret a literary work in such a way that the audience imaginatively senses characterization, setting, and action. Voice and body tension rather than movement are involved, thus eliminating the need for the many practice sessions that timing and action techniques require in the presentation of a play" (Laughlin and Latrobe 1990, 3). Traditionally, the primary focus in readers theatre is on an effective reading of the script rather than on a dramatic, memorized presentation. Generally, there are minimal props and movement on the stage, although with primary students, adding such touches enlivens the production and invites more active participation. The ease of incorporating readers theatre into the language arts program offers teachers an exciting way to enhance the program, especially in today's classrooms that emphasize a variety of reading and listening experiences.

The scripts in this collection were developed from folktales and fables that are familiar or have repetitive or cumulative lines. All scripts were evaluated with the Flesch-Kincaid readability scale and are grouped into sections with first-, second-, or third-grade readability levels (parts 1, 2, and 3, respectively). Although readability levels are given, the teacher and students are encouraged to sample all levels of scripts. Each script should be further evaluated by the teacher for features that will assist easy reading: familiarity, repetition, predictability, and so forth. Though children are not expected to memorize the lines in readers theatre, many children will have internalized the familiar story and will need only the slightest prompting from the script. Thus, paraphrasing by the reader is common and acceptable. Such success in reading and sharing is highly motivating for the beginning reader who appreciates the different forms of reading. After spending an entire morning exploring and practicing a script, one second-grader asked his teacher why they never had reading that day. She probed for a minute, then gently asked what they were doing as they prepared the script. He lit up in delight, "Oh, we *were* reading!"

The performance of readers theatre scripts also strengthens oral skills for readers and promotes active listening for students in the audience (Sloyer 1982, 4). Students explore literature in a new form, and the class can begin to analyze various treatments of the same or similar stories through use of the picture books listed with each script. An additional benefit is the pleasure of performing for parents or other classes and the ease of preparing for special days when a program is expected.

PREPARING THE SCRIPTS

Once scripts are chosen for reading, make enough copies for each character, plus an extra set or two for your use and a replacement copy. Because beginning readers may have difficulty keeping their place on the page, bold-faced character initials are included in the margin for the various parts (readability levels 1 and 2 only). Use highlighter markers to designate a character's picture within the copy. For example, the tortoise could be highlighted in blue each time it appears, the hare in green, and the narrator in orange. This helps readers track their parts and eases management of scripts in the event pages become mixed. Small numbers are included in the right margin for easy prompting by the teacher to a specific line.

Photocopied scripts will last longer if you use the three-hole punch (or copy them on prepunched paper) and place them in inexpensive folders. The folders can be color coordinated to the internal highlighting for each character's part. The title of the play can be printed on the outside of the folder, and scripts can be stored easily for the next reading. Preparing the scripts and folders is a good task for a volunteer parent or an older student helper. The preparation takes a minimum of initial attention and needs to be repeated only when a folder is lost.

GETTING STARTED

For the first experience with a readers theatre script, choose a script with many characters to involve as many students as possible. Gather the students informally, perhaps in a circle on the floor. If a picture book version of the chosen script is available, read it aloud to the students. Next, introduce the script version and explain that readers theatre does not mean memorizing a play and acting it out, but rather reading a script aloud with perhaps a few props and actions. Select volunteers to do the initial reading, allowing them an opportunity to review their parts before reading aloud. Other students could examine illustrated versions or brainstorm prop ideas and preview other scripts.

Before reading the first script, decide whether to choose parts after the reading or to introduce additional scripts to involve more students. A readers theatre workshop could be held periodically, with every student belonging to a group that prepares a script for presentation. A readers theatre festival could be planned for a special day when several short scripts are presented consecutively, with brief intermissions between each reading. Groups of tales could include the well-known Grimm tales, those by Hans Christian Andersen, the English tales, or a variety of animal tales. Consider these additional groupings drawn from this collection:

Aesop's fables: "Belling the Cat," "The Lion and the Mouse," "The Tortoise and the Hare," and "The Town Mouse and the Country Mouse."

Wolf tales: "The Three Little Pigs," "Little Red Riding Hood," and "The Wolf and the Seven Little Kids."

Royal tales: "Tom Tit Tot," "Cinderella," and "The Emperor's New Clothes."

Tales of distant lands: "Baba Yaga" (Russia), "The Half Chick" (Spain), "Kumba and Kambili" (Africa), and "The Peach Boy" (Japan).

Tales of clever children: "Baba Yaga," "The Little Boy Who Went to the North Wind," and "The Peach Boy."

Tales of foolishness: "The Three Wishes," "Tom Tit Tot," "The Emperor's New Clothes," and "Henny Penny."

Once the students have read the scripts and become familiar with new vocabulary, determine which students will read the various parts. In assigning roles, strive for a balance between males and females. Many roles are animals and may be read by either sex. Some parts are considerably more demanding than others, and students should be encouraged to volunteer for roles that will be comfortable for them. Once they are familiar with readers theatre, students should be encouraged to stretch and try a reading that is challenging. Though one goal for incorporating readers theatre is to develop and inspire competent readers, it is equally important that the students succeed and enjoy the literature.

PRESENTATION SUGGESTIONS

For readers theatre, readers traditionally stand—or sit on stools, chairs, or the floor—in a formal presentation style. The narrator may stand with the script placed on a music stand or lectern slightly off to one side. The readers may hold their scripts in black folders.

The position of the reader indicates the importance of the role. For example, the emperor in "The Emperor's New Clothes" would have a position in the front center of the stage, with the minor characters to the sides and slightly behind him. The tortoise and the hare from the Aesop fable would be positioned to the front and center, with the narrator and starter to the back and side.

Because these scripts are for beginning readers, it is important that the students are comfortable with the physical arrangement. It is assumed that the students will present more informally than in the traditional readers theatre style, perhaps adapting or enlivening the presentation. Therefore, a traditional arrangement for presenters is not provided with the scripts. Instead, a few general suggestions are supplied for each play. For example, readers of small parts may enter or leave the stage prior to and following their parts. Alternatively, readers may stand up for a reading and sit down for the remainder of the script.

Determining the presentation arrangement is a good cooperative activity for the readers. The arrangement should foster success; a student who cannot stand quietly for a long period of time should be allowed to sit on a chair, pillow, or the floor. The restless student with a short reading could remain on stage only for the duration of the reading. However, students may have fresh ideas for a different presentation, and their involvement should be fostered.

PROPS

Readers theatre traditionally has no, or few, props. However, simple costuming effects, such as a hat, apron, or scarf, plus a few props on stage will lend interest to the presentation. Shirlee Sloyer (1982, 58) suggests that a script can become a property: "a book, a fan, a gun, or any other object mentioned in the story." Suggestions for simple props or costuming are included; however, the students should be encouraged to decide how much or little to add to their production. Examining illustrated versions of the tales will give them many good ideas. However, for beginning readers, the use of props or actions may be overwhelming, and the emphasis should remain on the reading, rather than on an overly complicated presentation.

DELIVERY

In an effort to keep the scripts easy for beginning readers, no delivery suggestions are written within the scripts. Therefore, it is important to discuss with the students what will make the scripts come alive as they read. Primary students naturally incorporate voices into their creative play and should be encouraged to explore how this same practice will enhance their reading. Small groups that are working on individual plays should be invited to brainstorm delivery styles. A variety of warm-ups can help students with expression. For example, have the entire class respond to the following:

- discovering school has been canceled due to snow
- being grounded for something a sibling did
- learning a best friend is moving
- getting a new puppy or kitten
- being told there will be a big test every Monday
- discovering a sister ate your last piece of birthday cake
- having a genie or fairy appear with three wishes

In first experiences with presenting a script, it is tempting for students to keep their heads buried in the script, making sure they don't miss a line. Students should learn the material well enough to look up from the script during a presentation. Students can learn to use onstage focus, where they focus on each other during the presentation. This is most logical for characters who are interacting with each other. The use of offstage focus, where the presenters look directly into the eyes of the audience, is more logical for the narrator or characters that are uninvolved with onstage characters. An alternative is to have those students who do not interact with each other focus on a prearranged offstage location, such as the classroom clock, during delivery.

Simple actions can also be incorporated into readers theatre. Though primary students are generally less inhibited than older students, encourage presenters to use action by practicing pantomime in groups. If possible, have a mime come in for a presentation and some introductory instruction. Alternatively, introduce mime by having students try the following familiar actions: combing hair, brushing teeth, turning the pages of a book, eating an ice cream cone, making a phone call, falling asleep. Then select and try general activities drawn from the scripts: climbing, carrying items, putting a hat on and off, kneeling, and so forth. The actions need not be elaborate; characters can indicate falling asleep simply by closing their eyes. Although readers theatre uses minimal gestures and actions, they can brighten the presentations for both participants and audience.

Generally, the audience should be able to see the readers' facial expressions during the reading. Upon occasion a script lends itself to a character moving across the stage, facing each character while reading. In this event the characters should be turned enough that the audience can see the reader's face.

The use of music can enhance the delivery of the play. For "Kumba and Kambili," jungle drums may be used effectively during parts of the presentation. Royal music may be effective during the procession in "The Emperor's New Clothes." A bell may tinkle during "Belling the Cat." As with props and action, music should be added sparingly, as the emphasis should remain on the reading.

THE AUDIENCE

When students are part of the audience, they should understand their role. Caroline Feller Bauer (1992, 30) recommends that students should rehearse applauding and reacting appropriately to the script. Several of the plays include suggestions for involving the audience, such as providing sound effects during "The Three Billy Goats Gruff." Cue cards that prompt the audience to make noises can be incorporated into the production. Encourage students to find additional ways to involve the audience in the program.

BEYOND READERS THEATRE FOR
BEGINNING READERS

Once students have enjoyed the reading process involved in preparing and presenting readers theatre, the next logical step is to involve them in the writing process of creating their own scripts. The options for scripts are endless, and students will naturally want to translate a favorite story into a script. For an in-depth discussion of this process, consult part 1 of Shirlee Sloyer's *Readers Theatre: Story Dramatization in the Classroom*.

REFERENCES

Bauer, Caroline Feller. 1992. *Read for the Fun of It: Active Programming with Books for Children*. Illustrated by Lynn Gates Bredeson. Bronx, NY: H. W. Wilson.

Laughlin, Mildred Knight, and Kathy Howard Latrobe. 1990. *Readers Theatre for Children: Scripts and Script Development*. Englewood, CO: Teacher Ideas Press.

Sloyer, Shirlee. 1982. *Readers Theatre: Story Dramatization in the Classroom*. Urbana, IL: National Council of Teachers of English.

PART 1

BELLING THE CAT

SUMMARY

In this fable by Aesop, the mice are living contentedly until a cat disrupts their freedom. The mice meet and decide to attach a bell to a ribbon and tie it on the cat. However, no one is willing to tackle the task. *Reading level: 1.*

PRESENTATION SUGGESTIONS

This fable provides an opportunity to involve many students. Other Mice have several lines in unison, and there can be as many students as desired sharing this role. The formal staging could include Narrator, Mouse Leader, and Young Mouse positioned stage front. Alternatively, the staging could have Mouse Leader on the side, raised on a chair or stool, with the others loosely arranged as in a meeting. An additional (nonspeaking) role could be created for a cat who simply could prowl in the background.

PROPS

Most of the mice could wear pink and gray ears on a headband made of felt and reinforced with inter-facing. Mouse Leader could wear buttons or a hat to designate the role, and Wise Old Mouse could wear glasses. A ribbon and bell could be placed on stools onstage.

DELIVERY

Mouse Leader should have a strong voice. Other Mice can have squeaky and young voices. Young Mouse should sound young, and Wise Old Mouse should sound tentative. The audience could be prompted to contribute mouse and cat sounds with cue cards, and a bell could be rung softly when Young Mouse suggests belling the cat.

BOOKLIST

Calmenson, Stephanie, reteller. "Belling the Cat." In *The Children's Aesop*, 62. Illustrated by Robert Byrd. Honesdale, PA: Caroline House, 1992.
Calmenson has the mice tapping their tails when they have nothing to say. Share this version and compare it to the traditional story in the following collection.

Jacobs, Joseph, ed. "Belling the Cat." In *The Fables of Aesop*, 159. Illustrated by Richard Heighway. New York: Schocken Books, 1966.
This is a large collection of fables with a traditional treatment.

Paxton, Tom. "Belling the Cat." In *Belling the Cat and Other Aesop's Fables*. Illustrated by Robert Rayevsky. New York: Morrow Children's Books, 1990.
Paxton's verse and Rayevsky's color illustrations provide a lively version.

CHARACTERS

📖	Narrator	**HM**	Hungry Mouse
ML	Mouse Leader	**YM**	Young Mouse
OM	Other Mice (as many as preferred)	**WO**	Wise Old Mouse

BELLING THE CAT

 Narrator: There were many mice living happily together in a big, old house. One day a cat arrived. After the cat chased the mice for some days, the leader of the mice called the mice together.

ML **Mouse Leader:** My friends, we have a problem.   1

OM **Other Mice:** What is it?   2

ML **Mouse Leader:** It is that wicked cat! I am tired of being chased night and day.   3

HM **Hungry Mouse:** Me, too! I haven't had a crumb to eat since that beast came. I am so hungry!   4

OM **Other Mice:** Me, too! Me, too!   5

ML **Mouse Leader:** Well, we must come up with a plan. We have to be able to run about the house again.   6

OM **Other Mice:** A plan! A plan!   7

YM **Young Mouse:** I know what to do.   8

OM **Other Mice:** What? What?   9

YM **Young Mouse:** There is a bell in the corner of the kitchen and a ribbon in the bedroom. First we have to put the bell on the ribbon. Then we wait for the cat to fall asleep and tie the ribbon around his neck. When he moves, the bell will ring. We will be able to hear it and run away.   10

OM **Other Mice:** Hurray! Hurray!   11

ML **Mouse Leader:** That is a splendid plan. Let's do it!   12

WO **Wise Old Mouse:** Excuse me, please.   13

ML **Mouse Leader:** What is it, Old Mouse? We have no time to waste!   14

WO **Wise Old Mouse:** Who is going to tie the bell around the cat's neck?   15

ML **Mouse Leader:** Why, a volunteer, of course.   16

WO **Wise Old Mouse:** And who will volunteer?   17

 Narrator: The mice all looked at each other, waiting for someone to volunteer. No one did. And mice are still being caught by cats to this very day.

4

JACK AND THE BEANSTALK

SUMMARY

In this traditional English tale, Jack trades his cow for some magic beans. Jack climbs the beanstalk and finds the house of a giant and his wife. Jack steals their gold, their hen that lays golden eggs, and their singing harp. When the giant chases him, Jack chops down the beanstalk, and the giant falls to his death.
Reading level: 1.

PRESENTATION SUGGESTIONS

Although this is easy to read, it is much longer than many other scripts in this section. Because the old man has only a brief role, it may be wise to let that student exit or sit down after reading those lines. Similarly, Mother may want to stand for her first lines, sit during Jack's journeys to the giant's home, and stand for the ending lines.

PROPS

Mother may wear an apron or bonnet. Jack may wear a vest and cap or hat with a feather. The old man might wear a jacket, tie, or hat. The giant's wife might also wear an apron or have a broom. Suspenders and extra padding would enhance the giant's appearance.

DELIVERY

Jack's mother should sound appropriately motherly. Jack is rather ingenuous, but he is brave. His voice should vary depending on the circumstances he is in, such as when he begs the giant's wife for a bit of food. The old man should sound wheedling as he convinces Jack to trade for the beans. The giant's wife is usually cranky, and the giant is gruff. Students could participate in creating the THUMP, THUMP, THUMP! Ominous music could also introduce the giant each time he speaks.

BOOKLIST

Dahl, Roald. "Jack and the Beanstalk." In *Revolting Rhymes*, 21. Illustrated by Quentin Blake. New York: Bantam Skylark Books, 1986.
This amusing twist makes a good case for daily bathing. Before reading it aloud to older students, consider some minor editing in the event some lines might offend your listeners.

CHARACTERS

	Narrator	**OM**	Old Man
M	Mother	**W**	Wife
J	Jack	**G**	Giant

JACK AND THE BEANSTALK

 Narrator: A poor widow had one son named Jack and a cow named Milky-white. They lived well on the cow's milk. But one day it gave no more milk.

M **Mother:** Jack, Jack. What shall we do? 1

J **Jack:** Don't worry, Mother. I will get a job. 2

M **Mother:** But no one would take you the last time you tried. We must sell Milky-white. Take her to market today. Then we will make a new start. 3

J **Jack:** I'll sell her, and then we will see what to do next. 4

Narrator: Jack started down the road. Soon he met an old man.

OM **Old Man:** Good morning, lad. 5

J **Jack:** Good morning, sir. 6

OM **Old Man:** Where are you going? 7

J **Jack:** I'm going to market. I must sell our cow. 8

OM **Old Man:** Will you swap something for your cow? 9

J **Jack:** No, I must sell her. We need the money for a new start. 10

OM **Old Man:** Ah, this will give you the start you need. I'll trade you these beans for your cow. 11

J **Jack:** No, that would never do. My mother would be very unhappy. 12

OM **Old Man:** But these are magic beans. Plant them tonight. By morning they will grow up to the sky. 13

J **Jack:** Is that true? 14

OM **Old Man:** If it isn't true, you can have your cow back. 15

J **Jack:** That sounds fair. 16

Narrator: Jack traded his cow for the beans. He hurried home to tell his mother.

M **Mother:** That was quick, Jack. Did you get a good price? 17

J   **Jack:** Better than a good price!   18

M   **Mother:** How much then?   19

J   **Jack:** I traded Milky-white for these magic beans!   20

M   **Mother:** You are a fool! Those beans aren't magic. What will I do with you?   21

J   **Jack:** But Mother!   22

Narrator: Jack's mother threw the beans out the window and sent him to bed without his supper. The next morning when Jack woke up, his room looked strange. Instead of being filled with the usual morning sun, it was dark and shady. Jack got dressed and went to the window.

J   **Jack:** Goodness! That man was right! Those beans were magic. Look at that beanstalk!   23

Narrator: Jack leaned out the window and climbed right up the beanstalk, just like going up a ladder. When he reached the sky, he found a path. He walked along until he came to a big house. On the doorstep was a tall woman.

J   **Jack:** Good morning, ma'am.   24

W   **Wife:** Good morning, little boy.   25

J   **Jack:** I am hungry this morning. Would you be kind enough to give me some breakfast?   26

W   **Wife:** Breakfast! Ha! You'll *be* the breakfast if you don't go away. My husband is a giant, and he loves to eat boys on bread. Move on!   27

J   **Jack:** Oh please, ma'am. Couldn't I have just a little before I go? My mother sent me to bed with no supper last night.   28

W   **Wife:** All right, but you must be quick about it.   29

Narrator: Just as Jack was eating some bread and milk, the house began to shake. THUMP, THUMP, THUMP!

W   **Wife:** Oh, dear! My husband is home. You must hide. Quick! Into the oven!   30

G   **Giant:** Wife, cook these calves for me. But wait! What is that smell?   31

        Fee. Fi. Fo. Fum.

        I smell the blood of an Englishman.

W   **Wife:** There is no one here. Go wash up. I'll fix your breakfast.   32

Narrator: Jack was about to run away, but the woman told him to stay where he was.

Wife: Wait till after he eats. Then he will fall asleep.   33

Narrator: After breakfast the giant went to a big chest. He took out two bags of gold and began to count the coins. Soon he fell asleep. Jack sneaked out of the oven, grabbed one bag of coins, and ran for the beanstalk. He threw the gold down to the garden and climbed down till he got home.

Jack: Mother! Come see what I have! Gold! Those beans were magic!   34

Narrator: Jack and his mother lived on the gold for a long time. When it was almost gone, Jack decided to try his luck again. He climbed up the beanstalk and followed the path to the giant's house. There stood the tall woman on the doorstep again.

Jack: Good morning, ma'am.   35

Wife: Aren't you the bold one! Go away! My husband will eat you up.   36

Jack: Oh please, ma'am. Couldn't I have just a bite to eat before I move on?   37

Wife: You! Aren't you the one who came before? That was the day my husband lost a sack of gold.   38

Jack: I don't know about that. But I do know I am very hungry.   39

Narrator: Again she said she would give Jack a bite to eat. Just as before, the house began to shake. THUMP, THUMP, THUMP!

Wife: Oh, dear! My husband is home. You must hide. Quick! Into the oven.   40

Giant: Wife, cook these oxen for me. But what is that smell?   41
Fee. Fi. Fo. Fum.
I smell the blood of an Englishman.

Wife: Husband, there is no one here. I'll fix your breakfast.   42

Narrator: After breakfast the giant called to this wife.

Giant: Wife, bring me the hen that lays the golden eggs.   43

Narrator: After she brought the hen, the giant told it to lay. The hen laid an egg of gold. Again the giant fell asleep. Jack crept out of his hiding place, took the hen, and ran for the beanstalk. When Jack got home, he showed his mother the hen.

J   **Jack:**   Look, Mother! See what happens with this hen? Lay!   44

Narrator: The hen laid a golden egg. Every time Jack said "Lay!" the hen laid another golden egg. But even these riches did not satisfy Jack. He decided to try his luck again with the beanstalk. This time he did not go up to the giant's house, but hid until the wife came out to fetch some water. He crept into the house and hid behind the door. Soon he heard the THUMP, THUMP, THUMP! of the giant.

G   **Giant:**   Fee. Fi. Fo. Fum.   45

I smell the blood of an Englishman.

W   **Wife:**   Do you, dear? If it's that brat who stole the gold and hen, he's probably in the oven.   46

Narrator: They looked in the oven, but Jack wasn't there.

G   **Giant:**   Well, he isn't here. Bring me my golden harp, Wife.   47

Narrator: She brought him his harp. The giant told it to sing, and it played beautiful tunes. The giant fell asleep and began to snore. Jack slipped out from behind the door, sneaked over to the table, and grabbed the harp.

This time the harp called out, "Master, Master!" The giant woke up and saw Jack running away with his harp. Jack ran as fast as he could. When Jack got to the beanstalk, the giant was getting close. But the giant was afraid of climbing down the beanstalk.

The harp cried out again, "Master! Master!" The giant started down the beanstalk. Jack jumped the last few feet and ran for home.

J   **Jack:**   Mother! Mother! Bring the ax!   48

Narrator: Jack took the ax and began to chop at the beanstalk. With three swift chops, the beanstalk began to sway. The beanstalk fell over, and the giant fell to the earth. Jack and his mother were very happy to see the giant was dead.

J   **Jack:**   Mother, look at this treasure! A golden harp that can sing!   49

M   **Mother:**   You have done well, my son.   50

Narrator: Jack never replanted the beanstalk. From that day forward, Jack and his mother had their new start.

THE LION AND THE MOUSE

SUMMARY

In this fable from Aesop, a sleeping lion is awakened by a mouse using him as a playground. The lion agrees to let the mouse go. After the lion is captured by hunters, the mouse returns the favor by chewing through the lion's ropes.
Reading level: 1.

PRESENTATION SUGGESTIONS

Because this fable is very short, with only three characters, it could be paired with other fables in this section. Staging can be formal, with the characters sitting on stools or standing.

PROPS

The mouse could wear a headband with pink and gray felt ears reinforced with interfacing. The lion could have a swishing tail of rope and whiskers drawn on with eyeliner pencil. A tree or plant could be in the background.

DELIVERY

The mouse should have a small and squeaky voice. The lion should sound big and gruff.

BOOKLIST

Calmenson, Stephanie, reteller. "The Lion and the Mouse." In *The Children's Aesop*, 16. Illustrated by Robert Byrd. Honesdale, PA: Caroline House, 1992.
The illustration of the trapped lion demonstrates the challenge the mouse faced. Compare this to the script and the following version.

Carle, Eric, reteller. "The Lion and the Mouse." In *Twelve Tales from Aesop*, 26. New York: Philomel, 1980.
Carle's lion, dressed in suit, hat, and tie, provides a whimsical contrast to Calmenson's version.

CHARACTERS

 Narrator
L   Lion
M   Mouse

THE LION AND THE MOUSE

 Narrator: A lion was sound asleep. A mouse thought the lion would make a great place to play. He ran up the lion's back. Then he slid down the golden fur. He ran up and slid down again. The third time he ran up, the lion awoke with a roar.

L   **Lion:** ROAR! What is this? Who is playing on my back?   1

M   **Mouse:** Oops!   2

Narrator: The lion looked around. Seeing the mouse, he used his tail to pull the mouse to his mouth.

L   **Lion:** Looks like a tasty treat!   3

M   **Mouse:** Please forgive me, King Lion. I was only having some fun.   4

L   **Lion:** The fun is over for you!   5

M   **Mouse:** Wait! I won't be much of a meal for such a big lion. Let me go. Someday I will pay you back. Please?   6

L   **Lion:** Hmmph! I can't think how you could ever pay me back. But it is true. You are not even a mouthful. Be off with you then. Don't bother me again!   7

Narrator: The lion was soon asleep again. He did not hear some hunters creep up on him. Before he could even roar, they tied him to a tree. The hunters left to get a wagon to take the lion to the king. The lion roared his anger and fear at being trapped.

M   **Mouse:** That sounds like the lion! Why is he so upset? I'll go see what is wrong.   8

Narrator: The mouse found the lion tied to the tree.

M   **Mouse:** Be quiet, my friend. Now I can pay you back.   9

L   **Lion:** How is that? I need more help than a tiny mouse can give.   10

Narrator: But the mouse did not reply. He began to chew the ropes with his sharp little teeth. Soon the ropes fell away.

M   **Mouse:** Now you are free, King Lion. Run before the hunters return.   11

L   **Lion:** I may be free. But you have proved to me that little friends can be the best.   12

Narrator: From that day forth the lion and mouse were always friends.

THE OLD WOMAN AND HER PIG

SUMMARY

A woman finds a coin and decides to buy a pig in this cumulative English tale. The pig won't jump over the stile, and the woman solicits the help of various characters she meets on her way.

Reading level: 1.

PRESENTATION SUGGESTIONS

This script includes many characters. However, the woman does the bulk of the reading. With the exception of the last passage, the narrator's role is simple, a departure from most scripts. This is thus a good opportunity for a more tentative reader to assume the narrator's role. For more involvement on the part of the other characters and a resounding finish, the other characters and the audience could join in with the narrator during the reading of the last passage.

Staging could be formal, with the narrator and woman dominating the stage. An alternative is to have the minor characters step forward or stand up during their readings. For a more involved production, the characters could be in order from left to right across the stage. The woman could walk up to each character as they have their exchange, facing sideways to the audience. For the finale, all characters could face forward.

PROPS

Each character could be challenged to determine an appropriate prop. Suggestions include a hat for the narrator, an apron or bonnet for the woman, a collar or leash for the dog, a walking stick for the stick, wood for the fire, flowing ribbons for water, a bell for the ox, a butcher's hat or table knife for the butcher, rope for the rope, a rubber mouse or whiskers for the rat, a collar or catnip toy for the cat, and a bell or bucket for the cow.

DELIVERY

The many roles offer opportunities for interesting voices. Challenge the students to determine appropriate voices. Suggestions include a whiney voice for the woman, a barking voice for the dog, a sharp voice for the stick, a crackling voice for the fire, a flowing voice for the water, a deep voice for the ox, a rough voice for the butcher, an undulating voice for the rope, a squeaky voice for the rat, a meowing voice for the cat, and a mooing voice for the cow. The audience could join in as the rhyme accumulates.

BOOKLIST

Kent, Jack. *The Fat Cat*. New York: Scholastic, 1971.
    Compare the cumulative nature of this Danish folktale in which a cat keeps eating more items and people.

Rockwell, Anne, reteller. "The Old Woman and Her Pig." In *The Three Sillies and 10 Other Stories to Read Aloud*, 1. New York: Harper & Row, 1979.
    This is a simple retelling that is very similar to the script.

CHARACTERS

	Narrator	F	Fire	RO	Rope
WO	Woman	WA	Water	RA	Rat
D	Dog	O	Ox	CA	Cat
S	Stick	B	Butcher	CO	Cow

THE OLD WOMAN AND HER PIG

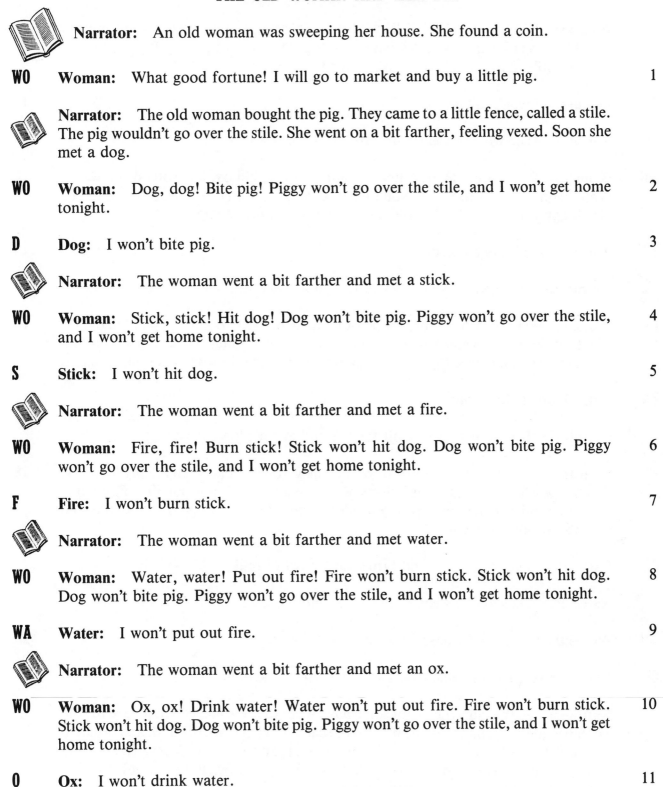

Narrator: An old woman was sweeping her house. She found a coin.

WO **Woman:** What good fortune! I will go to market and buy a little pig.   1

Narrator: The old woman bought the pig. They came to a little fence, called a stile. The pig wouldn't go over the stile. She went on a bit farther, feeling vexed. Soon she met a dog.

WO **Woman:** Dog, dog! Bite pig! Piggy won't go over the stile, and I won't get home tonight.   2

D **Dog:** I won't bite pig.   3

Narrator: The woman went a bit farther and met a stick.

WO **Woman:** Stick, stick! Hit dog! Dog won't bite pig. Piggy won't go over the stile, and I won't get home tonight.   4

S **Stick:** I won't hit dog.   5

Narrator: The woman went a bit farther and met a fire.

WO **Woman:** Fire, fire! Burn stick! Stick won't hit dog. Dog won't bite pig. Piggy won't go over the stile, and I won't get home tonight.   6

F **Fire:** I won't burn stick.   7

Narrator: The woman went a bit farther and met water.

WO **Woman:** Water, water! Put out fire! Fire won't burn stick. Stick won't hit dog. Dog won't bite pig. Piggy won't go over the stile, and I won't get home tonight.   8

WA **Water:** I won't put out fire.   9

Narrator: The woman went a bit farther and met an ox.

WO **Woman:** Ox, ox! Drink water! Water won't put out fire. Fire won't burn stick. Stick won't hit dog. Dog won't bite pig. Piggy won't go over the stile, and I won't get home tonight.   10

O **Ox:** I won't drink water.   11

Narrator: The woman went a bit farther and met a butcher.

WO   **Woman:**   Butcher, butcher! Kill ox! Ox won't drink water. Water won't put out   12
fire. Fire won't burn stick. Stick won't hit dog. Dog won't bite pig. Piggy won't go
over the stile, and I won't get home tonight.

B   **Butcher:**   I won't kill ox.   13

Narrator: The woman went a bit farther and met a rope.

WO   **Woman:**   Rope, rope! Hang butcher! Butcher won't kill ox. Ox won't drink water.   14
Water won't put out fire. Fire won't burn stick. Stick won't hit dog. Dog won't bite
pig. Piggy won't go over the stile, and I won't get home tonight.

RO   **Rope:**   I won't hang butcher.   15

Narrator: The woman went a bit farther and met a rat.

WO   **Woman:**   Rat, rat! Chew rope. Rope won't hang butcher. Butcher won't kill ox. Ox   16
won't drink water. Water won't put out fire. Fire won't burn stick. Stick won't hit
dog. Dog won't bite pig. Piggy won't go over the stile, and I won't get home tonight.

RA   **Rat:**   I won't chew rope.   17

Narrator: The woman went a bit farther and met a cat.

WO   **Woman:**   Cat, cat! Kill rat! Rat won't chew rope. Rope won't hang butcher.   18
Butcher won't kill ox. Ox won't drink water. Water won't put out fire. Fire won't
burn stick. Stick won't hit dog. Dog won't bite pig. Piggy won't go over the stile, and
I won't get home tonight.

CA   **Cat:**   If you go to the cow and bring me a bowl of milk, I will kill the rat.   19

Narrator: The woman went a bit farther and met a cow.

WO   **Woman:**   Cow, cow! I need some milk.   20

CO   **Cow:**   If you get me some hay, I will give you some milk.   21

Narrator: So the old woman got some hay. After the cow had eaten, it gave the old
woman some milk. She took the milk to the cat. The cat drank the milk and began to
kill rat. The rat began to chew rope. The rope began to hang butcher. The butcher
began to kill ox. The ox began to drink water. The water began to put out fire. The
fire began to burn stick. The stick began to hit dog. The dog began to bite pig. The
pig was so scared it jumped over the stile. And the old woman got home that night.

THE THREE BILLY GOATS GRUFF

SUMMARY

This Scandinavian tale features three goats who wish to eat grass on the other side of a bridge and a troll who wants to eat them up.
Reading level: 1.

PRESENTATION SUGGESTIONS

The repetitive language makes this script ideal for beginning readers. Staging can be formal, with the narrator and troll forward and the goats in order of appearance slightly behind. Alternatively, the narrator could be off to the side, the troll could be in the middle of the stage, and each goat could move past the troll as the part is read.

To involve more students, assign dual roles, with one set of characters serving as readers in a formal staging and the other set pantomiming the action in front of the readers. The play could be read a second time, with students trading roles.

PROPS

Each goat could have a bell, tail, or horns. The troll could have makeup to indicate fierce eyes, plus a wild wig, horns, or any other scary features.

DELIVERY

The goats should have voices suited to their individual sizes. The troll should sound very gruff. The part of the bridge, with its trip-trap noises, could be played by several students, or the narrator could direct the audience to join in with sound effects, perhaps using wood blocks or other rhythm instruments. Each subsequent trip-trap should be louder.

BOOKLIST

Alborough, Jez. *The Grass Is Always Greener*. New York: Dial Books for Young Readers, 1987.
This related story is about some sheep who follow Thomas to greener grass only to find that it is no better than what they had.

Hooks, William H. *The Gruff Brothers*. Illustrated by Pierre Cornuel. New York: Bantam Books, 1990.
This is an easy-to-read version that uses rebuses.

Stevens, Janet, reteller. *The Three Billy Goats Gruff*. San Diego, CA: Harcourt Brace Jovanovich, 1987.
These three goats plot to outsmart a frightening troll.

CHARACTERS

Narrator	**LB**	Little Billy Goat Gruff
B Bridge	**MB**	Middle Billy Goat Gruff
T Troll	**BB**	Big Billy Goat Gruff

THE THREE BILLY GOATS GRUFF

 Narrator: Once upon a time there were three billy goats. Their name was Gruff. They wanted to eat the green grass on the hillside to make themselves fat. On the way was a bridge over a stream. Under the bridge lived a mean, ugly troll. It had big eyes and a long nose. The youngest Billy Goat Gruff set off to cross the bridge.

B   **Bridge:**   Trip, trap! Trip, trap!   1

T   **Troll:**   Who's that trip-trapping over my bridge?   2

LB   **Little Billy Goat Gruff:**   It is I, the littlest Billy Goat Gruff. I'm going to the hillside to eat the green grass and make myself fat.   3

T   **Troll:**   Oh no you won't! For I am coming to eat you up!   4

LB   **Little Billy Goat Gruff:**   Oh please don't eat me! I am so little. Wait for the next Billy Goat Gruff. He is much bigger. He will make a much better meal for you.   5

T   **Troll:**   Well, then. Be off with you!   6

Narrator: So the littlest Billy Goat Gruff trip-trapped over the bridge. He began eating the green grass on the hillside. Soon the middle Billy Goat Gruff came across the bridge.

B   **Bridge:**   Trip, trap! Trip, trap! Trip, trap!   7

T   **Troll:**   Who's that trip-trapping over my bridge?   8

MB   **Middle Billy Goat Gruff:**   It is I, the middle Billy Goat Gruff. I'm going to the hillside to eat the green grass and make myself fat.   9

T   **Troll:**   Oh no you won't! For I am coming to eat you up!   10

MB   **Middle Billy Goat Gruff:**   Oh please don't eat me! I am not so big. Wait for the big Billy Goat Gruff. He is so much bigger. He will make a much better meal for you.   11

T   **Troll:**   Well, then. Be off with you!   12

Narrator: So the middle Billy Goat Gruff trip-trapped over the bridge. He began eating the green grass on the hillside. Soon the big Billy Goat Gruff came across the bridge.

B   **Bridge:**   TRIP, TRAP! TRIP, TRAP! TRIP, TRAP! TRIP, TRAP!   13

T   **Troll:**   Who's that TRIP-TRAPPING over my bridge?   14

BB   **Big Billy Goat Gruff:**   IT IS I, THE BIG BILLY GOAT GRUFF! I'm going to the   15
hillside to eat the green grass and make myself even fatter.

T   **Troll:**   Oh no you won't! For I am coming to eat you up!   16

BB   **Big Billy Goat Gruff:**   Then come on up!   17

For I have two horns.

I'll poke out your eyeballs!

I'll crush all your bones.

 Narrator: The troll flew at the big Billy Goat Gruff. But the big Billy Goat Gruff butted and poked him just as he promised. The big Billy Goat Gruff threw the troll into the stream and went on up the hillside. There the three Billy Goats Gruff ate and ate and ate. They got so fat they could hardly walk home. So ...

Snip, snap, snout.

This tale's told out.

THE THREE LITTLE PIGS

SUMMARY

This is the familiar English tale of the three pigs who build their houses of straw, sticks, and bricks. The wolf blows down the houses of straw and sticks, eating the pigs. But the third pig outsmarts him.
Reading level: 1.

PRESENTATION SUGGESTIONS

The familiar story and repetitive lines make this a comfortable script for the earliest readers. The presentation can be formal, with the pigs and wolf at the front of the stage. Because they have only one line each, the merchants could exit or sit down after their lines.

In an alternative presentation, the merchants could approach the pigs, leave the straw, sticks, or bricks, and exit the stage. Later the wolf could approach each pig in turn, with the first and second pigs sitting to indicate being eaten. When the third pig outsmarts the wolf, it could also sit. Remember that all characters can be male or female in this play.

PROPS

Have the merchants carry the straw, sticks, or bricks. The pigs can wear vests or hats, with freckles added with makeup. The wolf can have a tail, makeup for whiskers and mean eyes, or a stuffed shirt to indicate big lungs.

DELIVERY

The three pigs' voices could sound increasingly mature, from the first to the third. The wolf should sound gruff. For more audience involvement have a second reading and invite the audience to join in with "Not by the hair of my chinny chin chin" and "Then I'll huff and I'll puff and I'll blow your house down!"

BOOKLIST

Claverie, Jean, reteller. *The Three Little Pigs*. Translated and adapted by Elizabeth D. Crawford. New York: North-South Books, 1989.
Claverie's soft illustrations are alive with movement.

Dahl, Roald. "The Three Little Pigs." In *Revolting Rhymes*, 47. Illustrated by Quentin Blake. New York: Bantam Skylark Books, 1986.
This outrageous poem should be shared after reading "Little Red Riding Hood" in the same collection. Students will enjoy not only the twists Dahl brings, but also his interplay with the two stories.

Hooks, William H. *The Three Little Pigs and the Fox*. Illustrated by S. D. Schindler. New York: Macmillan, 1989.
This version set in Appalachia is a humorous contrast to the familiar versions.

Scieszka, Jon. *The True Story of the 3 Little Pigs by A. Wolf*. Illustrated by Lane Smith. New York: Viking Kestrel, 1989.
A. Wolf tells his side of the story in this amusing twist on the traditional tale. Children will enjoy the fresh treatment.

CHARACTERS

	Narrator	**3P**	Third Pig	**3M**	Third Merchant
1P	First Pig	**1M**	First Merchant	**W**	Wolf
2P	Second Pig	**2M**	Second Merchant		

THE THREE LITTLE PIGS

Narrator: Three pigs left their mother's house. They had to build their own houses before winter came. The first pig met a merchant carrying some straw.

1P   **First Pig:** Please could I have some of your straw? I need to build a house before winter.   1

2P & 3P   **Second Pig and Third Pig:** Straw! That will not be very strong!   2

1P   **First Pig:** It will do just fine!   3

1M   **First Merchant:** Here is your straw, then.   4

Narrator: The first pig built his house of straw. Soon the second pig met a man carrying some sticks.

2P   **Second Pig:** Please could I have some of your sticks? I need to build a house before winter.   5

3P   **Third Pig:** Sticks! That will not be very strong!   6

2P   **Second Pig:** Sticks are stronger than straw. It will do just fine!   7

2M   **Second Merchant:** Here are your sticks, then.   8

Narrator: The second pig built his house of sticks. Soon the third pig met a man carrying some bricks.

3P   **Third Pig:** Please could I have some of your bricks? I need to build a house before winter.   9

1P & 2P   **First Pig and Second Pig:** Bricks! You will have to have mortar for a house of bricks. And it will take you so long to build it!   10

3P   **Third Pig:** It will take some work. But it will be strong. And I have time before winter comes.   11

3M   **Third Merchant:** Here are your bricks, then.   12

Narrator: So the third pig built his house of bricks. Soon it was nearly winter. A hungry wolf needed to fatten up before the snow fell. He came to the house of straw the first pig had built.

W   **Wolf:** Little pig, little pig.

Let me come in!   13

23

1P   **First Pig:**   Not by the hair of my chinny chin chin.   14

W   **Wolf:**   Then I'll huff and I'll puff.   15

      And I'll blow your house down!

 Narrator: The wolf blew the house down. Then he ate the pig. He went down the road and saw the house of straw built by the second pig.

W   **Wolf:**   Little pig, little pig.   16

      Let me come in!

2P   **Second Pig:**   Not by the hair of my chinny chin chin.   17

W   **Wolf:**   Then I'll huff and I'll puff.   18

      And I'll blow your house down.

 Narrator: The wolf blew that house down. Then he ate the second pig. Feeling happily full, he went down the road. He saw the house of the third pig. He decided that dessert would be just right.

W   **Wolf:**   Little pig, little pig.   19

      Let me come in!

3P   **Third Pig:**   Not by the hair of my chinny chin chin.   20

W   **Wolf:**   Then I'll huff and I'll puff.   21

      And I'll blow your house down!

 Narrator: The wolf blew. And blew. And huffed. And puffed. But the third pig's house was too strong. The wolf couldn't blow it down.

W   **Wolf:**   Hmm. There has to be a way. Maybe I can't blow down the house. But I   22 can surely get inside.

 Narrator: The wolf returned home for a rope. He went back to the third pig's house and threw the rope around the chimney. He pulled himself up to the roof. He used the rope to let himself down the chimney. But little did he know just how smart that pig was. The third pig had filled a pot with water and heated it on his fire. The wolf landed with a splash in the boiling water. That was the end of the wolf. But the pig lived to a ripe old age.

THE TORTOISE AND THE HARE

SUMMARY

In this fable by Aesop, the hare brags that he can win any race. When the tortoise challenges him, the overconfident hare naps and consequently loses the race.
Reading level: 1.

PRESENTATION SUGGESTIONS

Consider combining the reading of this and other short scripts in this section. Staging can be formal, with characters sitting on stools or standing. To involve more students, consider assigning dual roles with the second set of characters pantomiming the fable in front of the readers.

PROPS

Consider giving the hare long ears and tennis shoes. The tortoise could wear padded clothes and boots to indicate heaviness. The starter could wear a stopwatch around his or her neck.

DELIVERY

The hare should speak boastfully and quickly. The tortoise should speak quietly and deliberately. The starter should have a commanding voice. The audience could be directed to join in with "On your marks. Get set. GO!"

BOOKLIST

Calmenson, Stephanie, reteller. "The Hare and the Tortoise." In *The Children's Aesop*, 4. Illustrated by Robert Byrd. Honesdale, PA: Caroline House, 1992.
    Students will enjoy the rich illustration of the tortoise, who appears to relish his progress in the race.

Castle, Caroline, reteller. *The Hare and the Tortoise.* Illustrated by Peter Weevers. New York: Dial Books for Young Readers, 1985.
    Compare this book-length version illustrated with Weever's elegant watercolors to the following book by Janet Stevens.

Stevens, Janet, adapter. *The Tortoise and the Hare.* New York: Holiday House, 1984.
    Stevens has expanded this tale into a book-length version with amusing touches, such as the tortoise's tennis shoes.

CHARACTERS

 Narrator
H   Hare
T   Tortoise
S   Starter

THE TORTOISE AND THE HARE

 Narrator: Once there was a tortoise and a hare. The tortoise was slow and careful. The hare did everything fast. He loved to brag about his speed.

H **Hare:** I am so fast! I have never been beaten in a race. There isn't anyone who can beat me! In fact, no one is brave enough to try. 1

T **Tortoise:** I am brave enough. I will race you. 2

H **Hare:** You! That is a fine joke. I could run circles around you and still win the race! 3

T **Tortoise:** You should save your bragging until you've won. 4

H **Hare:** Let's race then! 5

Narrator: The tortoise and the hare agreed on the race course. They would race on the path that led through the woods. All the animals lined up to watch.

S **Starter:** Quiet! Quiet! It is time for the race. You know the rules. The first to cross the finish line is the winner. Tortoise, are you ready? 6

T **Tortoise:** Yes, I am. 7

S **Starter:** Hare, are you ready? 8

H **Hare:** Of course! This will be a quick race! 9

S **Starter:** On your marks. Get set. GO! 10

Narrator: The tortoise got off to a steady start. The hare left a trail of dust as he raced off down the path.

T **Tortoise:** Oh, dear! Look at the hare go. I shouldn't have been so brave. But there is no going back, only forward. 11

Narrator: The tortoise plodded on, hardly lifting his head to look down the path. Meanwhile, the hare stopped to look back for the tortoise. He waited and waited but didn't see him.

H **Hare:** This is too boring. I think I'll take a bit of a nap. That tortoise won't be along for hours. 12

Narrator: The tortoise plodded on. The hare slept on. Finally, the tortoise neared the finish line. His animal friends began to cheer.

H **Hare:** What? What is all that noise? It must be time to finish the race. 13

 Narrator: But it was too late for the hare. The tortoise crossed the finish line just as the hare came around the last turn. As the animals cheered, the tortoise had only one thing to say to the hare.

T **Tortoise:** Slow and steady wins the race. 14

THE TOWN MOUSE AND THE COUNTRY MOUSE

SUMMARY

Two mice who are cousins visit each other's homes, finding that both city and country have their drawbacks. This is a short, easy fable by Aesop.
Reading level: 1.

PRESENTATION SUGGESTIONS

This familiar tale is especially suitable for beginning readers. Staging can be formal, with the two mice taking center stage. The cook could enter and exit for her reading.

Alternatively, dual roles could be assigned, with some students pantomiming the play while others read. Because the mice are often thought of as males, it would be suitable to have both a girl and a boy in the mouse roles, and perhaps for one portrayal to use girls for both mice. The script should be revised accordingly.

PROPS

The town mouse should be in dress clothes. The country mouse can be dressed casually, perhaps in tennis shoes, T-shirt, and jeans. The town mouse could have an elegant suitcase nearby, while the country mouse might have a battered bag or a bundle on a stick. The cook could wear a hat or apron. The cat might have felt ears, whiskers, tail, or collar.

DELIVERY

The town mouse should sound sophisticated and elegant and the country mouse simple and countrified. The cook should sound outraged, and the cat should sound appropriately eager to eat the mice.

BOOKLIST

Kent, Jack. "The Town Mouse and the Country Mouse." In *Jack Kent's Fables of Aesop*, 44. New York: Parents' Magazine Press, 1972.
Kent's simple version and drawings may suggest props to students.

Paxton, Tom. "Town Mouse and Country Mouse." In *Belling the Cat and Other Aesop's Fables*. Illustrated by Robert Rayevsky. New York: Morrow Children's Books, 1990.
Paxton's verse and Rayevsky's illustrations provide an amusing interpretation of this fable.

Stevens, Janet, adapter. *The Town Mouse and the Country Mouse*. New York: Holiday House, 1987.
Stevens's illustrations are rich and detailed in this book-length version.

CHARACTERS

 Narrator

TM   Town Mouse

CM   Country Mouse

C   Cook

MC   Mouser the Cat

THE TOWN MOUSE AND THE COUNTRY MOUSE

 Narrator: One day the town mouse decided to visit his cousin in the country. The mice had a good chat. They had a breakfast of nuts and seeds. For lunch they had a picnic of nuts and seeds. The country mouse baked nuts and seeds for dinner. The town mouse soon tired of eating nuts and seeds.

TM   **Town Mouse:** Cousin, come visit me in the city. I am tired of this simple food. I promise you that we will dine on the finest meats and cakes.   1

CM   **Country Mouse:** That sounds splendid! When shall we go?   2

TM   **Town Mouse:** Let's go now. I am ready to be home.   3

Narrator: The country mouse packed a simple bag. After some time they came near the city.

TM   **Town Mouse:** We are almost home! I will be so happy to have real food!   4

Narrator: The mice came to a huge house. The town mouse led the country mouse to a small opening in the bricks in the back.

TM   **Town Mouse:** Shhh! Now you must be as quiet as a whisper.   5

CM   **Country Mouse:** Why?   6

TM   **Town Mouse:** Never mind. Just be quiet.   7

Narrator: The town mouse led the country mouse into the dining room. They scampered up the table. The table was littered with the remains of a fine feast.

TM   **Town Mouse:** Now you see how I eat! Help yourself to anything you wish.   8

CM   **Country Mouse:** This is great! No wonder you wanted to come home.   9

Narrator: The mice were enjoying second helpings when the kitchen door opened.

C   **Cook:** Eeeek! Mice! Now there are two! Where is that pesky cat? Mouser! Mouser! Where are you?   10

TM   **Town Mouse:** Time to run, cousin. Follow me!   11

Narrator: The town mouse led the country mouse to a hole under the floor.

CM   **Country Mouse:** Who was that?   12

TM   **Town Mouse:**   That is the cook. Don't worry about her. She is harmless. She'll go   13
back to the kitchen. Then we'll have dessert.

Narrator: Soon it was quiet again. The town mouse led the country mouse back to
the dining table.

TM   **Town Mouse:**   Eat, my friend, eat. You won't find such sweet cakes in the country.   14

Narrator: But just then, Mouser the Cat leaped onto the table. One paw landed on
the country mouse's tail.

MC   **Mouser the Cat:**   What have I here? Looks like dessert! Mrowr!   15

TM   **Town Mouse:**   Run, cousin! Run! Meet me below!   16

Narrator: But the country mouse had seen enough. He twitched his tail away from
the cat. Then he darted toward the door.

CM   **Country Mouse:**   No thanks, cousin! If this is life in the city, it is not for me. I'll   17
take my seeds and nuts any day. Good-bye! From now on, you come and visit me!

Narrator: And that is why the town mouse has to go to the country to see his
cousin.

PART 2

5

THE BREMEN TOWN MUSICIANS

SUMMARY

In this German tale, a donkey running away from certain death plans to be a musician in the city. On the way to Bremen he meets various other down-and-out animals who decide to join him. While seeking shelter for the night, they discover and scare off a house of robbers. They live comfortably together thereafter.

Reading level: 2.

PRESENTATION SUGGESTIONS

The themes of survival and good over evil are strong components of this play. The staging can be formal, with the characters sitting on stools or standing while reading their parts. Nonspeaking parts could be included for the other robbers, with all of them exiting the stage when frightened away.

For a variation, challenge the students to extend the script by including more animals. Encourage them to determine how they would participate as musicians and in the resolution of the plot when the robbers are finally ousted.

PROPS

The animals could have distinguishing features: donkey ears and tail, a dog collar or tail, cat whiskers or tail, a wattle or feathers, and a cap and rough clothes for the robber leader.

DELIVERY

The animals should have voices suited to their roles. All the animals could punctuate their comments with a bray, woof, meow, or cock-a-doodle-doo. Rhythm instruments such as a sand block, wood block, triangle, and whistle could be matched to the animal sounds. The robber leader should sound alternately sneaky and scared. Cue cards could prompt the audience to provide the appropriate animal noises.

BOOKLIST

Crossley-Holland, Kevin. "The Bremen Town Musicians." In *The Fox and the Cat: Kevin Crossley-Holland's Animal Tales from Grimm*, 54. Illustrated by Susan Varley. New York: Lothrop, Lee & Shepard, 1985.
Students will enjoy comparing this version to the script.

Rockwell, Anne, reteller. "The Bremen Town Musicians." In *The Three Sillies and 10 Other Stories to Read Aloud*, 52. New York: Harper & Row, 1979.
The simple text and illustrations make this a good introduction to the script.

CHARACTERS

📖	Narrator	C	Cat
DK	Donkey	R	Rooster
DO	Dog	RL	Robber Leader

THE BREMEN TOWN MUSICIANS

 Narrator: There once was a donkey who worked hard for his master. But as he grew old, he grew weak. The donkey knew that the master was thinking of getting rid of him.

DK   **Donkey:** I will run away and go to the city of Bremen. My body is weak, but my voice is strong. I will find work as a singer.   1

Narrator: The donkey ambled toward the city. Soon he saw a dog.

DK   **Donkey:** Why are you panting so hard, my friend?   2

DO   **Dog:** Ah, I am old and weak. My master was going to be rid of me. So I ran away. Now I wonder, how will I make my way?   3

DK   **Donkey:** I am going to the city of Bremen to be a singer. Come with me. I know that dogs can howl. Perhaps you can be a musician as well.   4

DO   **Dog:** You are kind, sir. I will be happy to join you.   5

Narrator: The donkey and dog set off together. Soon they came on a cat sitting in the middle of the road.

DK   **Donkey:** Why do you look so sad, dear cat?   6

C   **Cat:** It is hard to be happy when one is soon to die. I am too old to catch mice. My mistress was about to drown me this very day. But I ran away. But how will I find food if I cannot catch mice?   7

DK   **Donkey:** All cats know how to sing at night. Come with us. We will find good jobs as musicians in the city of Bremen.   8

C   **Cat:** What a grand idea! Thank you for your kindness.   9

Narrator: The cat joined the donkey and dog. Soon they walked by a farm-yard. A rooster flew up on the fence.

R   **Rooster:** Cock-a-doodle-doo!   10

DK   **Donkey:** What a fine voice! Why do you crow?   11

R   **Rooster:** This is how I woke the family each day. But the cook says I am soon to be Sunday stew. What shall I do?   12

DK   **Donkey:** No stew pot for you! Come with us to the city of Bremen. We will find jobs as musicians. Maybe we will give a concert with the four of us!   13

R   **Rooster:** I would be proud to be a musician with you! Thank you!   14

Narrator: The rooster joined the donkey, dog, and cat. They walked along till nighttime, but the city was still far away. They looked for a dry place in the woods to rest. They found a place under a big tree. Before going to sleep the rooster flew into the tree to look around.

R   **Rooster:** I see a light a ways off. Perhaps there is a house.   15

DK   **Donkey:** Let's go to it. It will be better than sleeping in the open. Perhaps there will be a bit of hay for me.   16

DO   **Dog:** Perhaps there will be a bone for me!   17

C   **Cat:** Perhaps some milk for me!   18

R   **Rooster:** And I could find some corn!   19

Narrator: The rooster led them to the light. When they got to the house, the donkey peeked in the window.

DK   **Donkey:** Oh dear! This is a house of robbers!   20

DO   **Dog:** How do you know?   21

DK   **Donkey:** There are guns all about. Money is piled on the floors. And the robbers are eating and drinking at a fine table with gold dishes.   22

R   **Rooster:** I would like some of that fine food.   23

C & DO   **Cat and Dog:** So would I!   24

DK   **Donkey:** We must think of a plan.   25

Narrator: So the donkey, dog, cat, and rooster discussed what they must do. Soon the donkey stood on his hind legs. The dog got on his shoulders. The cat got on the dog's back. And the rooster flew up to the back of the cat.

DK   **Donkey:** Hee haw! Hee haw!   26

DO   **Dog:** Bow wow! Bow wow!   27

C   **Cat:** Meow! Meow!   28

R   **Rooster:** Cock-a-doodle-doo!   29

Narrator: The robbers looked out the window. All they could hear was this horrible noise. They ran out of the house, fearing for their lives.

**DK, DO,
C, & R**   **Donkey, Dog, Cat, and Rooster:**   Hurray! Hurray! Let's eat!   30

Narrator: The four musicians sat down at the table. They ate and ate. Soon they found familiar places to sleep. Meanwhile, the robbers saw the lights go out.

RL   **Robber Leader:**   Maybe we left too fast. Stay here. I will go find out if there is   31
anything to fear.

Narrator: The leader of the robbers crept back to the house. He found a candle and some matches. The cat, curled up by the fireplace, woke up. Its eyes shone as it watched the robber. The robber thought the eyes were glowing coals. He lit a match and tried to touch the coals with it. The cat flew at his face, spitting and scratching him. This woke the dog, who was lying by the door. It bit the robber's leg as he ran out. The donkey in the yard gave him a kick with his hind foot. And the rooster on the roof crowed its loudest.

R   **Rooster:**   Cock-a-doodle-doo!   32

RL   **Robber Leader:**   We can't live there any more. There is a witch in the kitchen   33
with hot breath and long nails. A man by the door stabbed me in the leg. A giant
in the yard hit me with a club. And a fellow on the roof shouted, "Give him up to
me!"

Narrator: The musicians never went to the city. But they had so many riches in
the robbers' house that they never went without again.

GOLDILOCKS AND THE THREE BEARS

SUMMARY

This English tale is about a family of bears that leaves the house for a walk in the woods while their porridge cools. A young girl, Goldilocks, explores their house while they are gone, eating their porridge, breaking a chair, and sleeping on Baby Bear's bed.
Reading level: 2.

PRESENTATION SUGGESTIONS

Students enjoy this familiar tale of discovery and escape. The characters can be placed in order of appearance on the stage. In an alternative arrangement, the bears can exit during Goldilocks's exploration and return at the resolution. Upon her discovery, Goldilocks can run off the stage.

This script lends itself well to a dual presentation, with a second set of characters pantomiming the play during its reading. Parts can be traded to allow for more participation.

PROPS

The bears can be dressed in old-fashioned trousers and suspenders. Goldilocks can be dressed for outdoor play. For a more elaborate production with the pantomime characters, a simple kitchen with bowls and chairs can be set up, with pillows representing the three beds.

DELIVERY

The bears should have voices appropriate to their sizes and roles. Goldilocks should sound young and innocent. For more audience participation, have students practice joining in on the bears' lines after they return to the house (e.g., "Someone's been sitting in my chair," and so forth). Rhythm instruments could be used to signal the departure and arrival of the bears.

BOOKLIST

Dahl, Roald, "Goldilocks and the Three Bears." In *Revolting Rhymes*, 31. Illustrated by Quentin Blake. New York: Bantam Skylark Books, 1986.
  Preread this irreverent, amusing treatment before sharing it with older students.

Stevens, Janet, reteller. *Goldilocks and the Three Bears*. New York: Holiday House, 1986.
  Stevens's illustrations colorfully highlight this traditional version.

Watts, Bernadette, reteller. *Goldilocks and the Three Bears*. New York: North-South Books, 1984.
  Watts has provided a simple retelling with lovely illustrations.

CHARACTERS

📖	Narrator	PB	Papa Bear
BB	Baby Bear	G	Goldilocks
MB	Mama Bear		

GOLDILOCKS AND THE THREE BEARS

 Narrator: Once upon a time there were three bears. One was Baby Bear, the smallest. The middle-size bear was Mama Bear. The biggest bear was Papa Bear. They lived together in a house in the woods. One day Mama Bear made porridge for breakfast. They all sat down to eat.

BB   **Baby Bear:**   Ouch! This porridge is too hot!   1

MB   **Mama Bear:**   You are right, Baby Bear. What shall we do until it is cool?   2

PB   **Papa Bear:**   Let's take a walk in the woods. When we come back, it will be just right.   3

Narrator: The bear family left the porridge cooling on the table. They walked into the woods, enjoying the fresh morning air. While they were away, a little girl named Goldilocks was also walking in the woods. Her mother had sent her on an errand. She walked by the bear's house and smelled the porridge.

G   **Goldilocks:**   Oooh. What smells so good? I think I'll just take a quick peek.   4

Narrator: Goldilocks looked in the window and saw the porridge on the table. She gave a push to the door and walked right in.

G   **Goldilocks:**   Look at this big bowl of porridge. I'll have to try it. Oh dear. This is just too hot. Maybe this middle-size bowl is better. No, it is just a bit too cold. I'll try this little bowl. Oh yes! This is just right!   5

Narrator: Goldilocks ate every bite of Baby Bear's porridge. Then she began to look around the house. She noticed the three chairs for the bears.

G   **Goldilocks:**   Look at those chairs! I think I'll try the big one first. Goodness! This chair is much too hard for me. Maybe the middle-size chair is better. No. Too soft. I bet this little one will be just right.   6

Narrator: But when Goldilocks sat down, the little chair broke right out from under her. That made her very cross. She decided to look upstairs. She found the bears' three beds.

G   **Goldilocks:**   Those beds look very inviting. I think I'll rest my eyes for just a bit. I'll try the big bed first. Oh my! This is much too high for me. Perhaps the middle-size bed is better. No, this bed is too soft. I'll try the little one. Yes, this is just right.   7

Narrator: And with that, Goldilocks fell fast asleep. Very soon, the bears came back from their walk.

BB   **Baby Bear:**   Look, Father! The door is open!   8

MB **Mama Bear:** Let's go in carefully.   9

Narrator: Papa Bear was the first to see that someone had been eating the porridge.

PB **Papa Bear:** SOMEONE HAS BEEN EATING MY PORRIDGE!   10

Narrator: Mama Bear saw that some of her porridge was gone also.

MB **Mama Bear:** Oh dear. Someone has been eating my porridge as well!   11

Narrator: Then baby bear saw that his bowl was empty.

BB **Baby Bear:** Someone has been eating my porridge! And it's all gone!   12

Narrator: The bears began to look around the house. Papa Bear saw that the cushion was off his chair.

PB **Papa Bear:** SOMEONE HAS BEEN SITTING IN MY CHAIR!   13

Narrator: Then Mama Bear saw that someone had moved her shawl.

MB **Mama Bear:** Someone has been sitting in my chair, too!   14

Narrator: Then Baby Bear saw what was left of his chair.

BB **Baby Bear:** Someone has been sitting in my chair! And it's all broken!   15

Narrator: The bears went upstairs, looking around carefully. Papa Bear was first to see that his blanket was crumpled.

PB **Papa Bear:** SOMEONE HAS BEEN SLEEPING IN MY BED!   16

Narrator: Then Mama Bear saw that her pillow was mussed.

MB **Mama Bear:** Someone has been sleeping in my bed, too!   17

Narrator: Then Baby Bear spotted Goldilocks, sound asleep in his bed.

BB **Baby Bear:** Someone has been sleeping in my bed! And there she is!   18

Narrator: Goldilocks woke with a start. Seeing the three bears, she leaped from the bed, ran down the stairs, and dashed out the door. Goldilocks was so scared she ran straight home. The bears still took their morning walk when the porridge was too hot. But they made sure to lock their door.

THE HALF CHICK

SUMMARY

This is a Spanish tale of a chick born with half a body. The chick does not let its disability stop it from journeying to the king's castle. But on the way, it chooses to ignore pleas for help from the water, fire, and wind. When it is thrown into the cooking pot for broth, the water, fire, and wind will not help it. The half chick is relegated to spending its days as a weather vane atop a church in Madrid.
Reading level: 2.

PRESENTATION SUGGESTIONS

Discuss what a weather vane is with students before sharing this tale. The elements of water, fire, and wind are also important features. Be sure students are comfortable with the pronunciation of Medio Pollito: May'-de-o Po-yee'-to. Staging should feature Medio Pollito and the elements. The mother hen could exit after her reading.

PROPS

Costume touches could include a yellow shirt for the chick, a blue shirt for the water, an orange shirt for the fire, a white shirt for the wind, and a hat and apron for the cook. Props could include a pot and a weather vane placed onstage.

DELIVERY

Mother Hen should sound motherly and kind. Medio Pollito should sound successively brave, haughty, and pleading. The water, fire, and wind should sound pleading and later regretful. The cook should sound pleased with finding the chicken for her broth. Musical instruments could be used to indicate the water, fire, and wind.

BOOKLIST

Lobel, Arnold. "The Young Rooster." In *Fables*, 37. New York: Harper & Row, 1980.
   This is a different story with a happier ending and an interesting depiction of the rooster in a weather vane position. Use it to discuss how roosters came to be used as weather vanes.

CHARACTERS

📖	Narrator	**F**	Fire
MH	Mother Hen	**WI**	Wind
MP	Medio Pollito	**C**	Cook
WA	Water		

THE HALF CHICK

Narrator: There once was a Spanish hen who had many chickens. They were all fine, fat chicks, except the youngest. This chick looked like it was cut in half. It had one leg, one wing, one eye, half a head, and half a beak.

MH   **Mother Hen:** You poor chick. You will never grow up to rule a farmyard like your brothers. But never mind. You will always be here to keep me company.   1

Narrator: She called the chick Medio Pollito, Spanish for "half-chick." But she soon found that he was unlike his brothers in other ways as well as his appearance. His brothers always came when she called. But Medio Pollito loved to roam. He used his one leg to kick and hop his way around the yard. When she called, he would pretend he didn't hear her with his one good ear. One day he came home after a long exploration.

MP   **Medio Pollito:** Mother, I am tired of this dull farmyard. I am going to Madrid to see the king.   2

MH   **Mother Hen:** Don't be silly! You can't go to Madrid. It is much too far. Forget such a journey. Just stay home with me.   3

MP   **Medio Pollito:** I am sorry, Mother. I must go. When I have my yard in the king's palace, you can come visit me.   4

MH   **Mother Hen:** Medio Pollito, please stay. I will miss you so.   5

Narrator: But Medio Pollito was on his way. He walked a long way. He passed a stream that called to him.

WA   **Water:** Oh, Medio Pollito, please help me! I am choking from these weeds. Please come clear them away.   6

MP   **Medio Pollito:** Help you? You can help yourself! I am off to Madrid to see the king!   7

Narrator: And Medio Pollito hopped and kicked down the road. Soon he came to a fire that called to him.

F   **Fire:** Oh, Medio Pollito, please help me! I am burning so low. Please put some sticks and leaves upon me so I won't die.   8

MP   **Medio Pollito:** Help you? You can help yourself! I am off to Madrid to see the king!   9

Narrator: And Medio Pollito hopped and kicked down the road. The next morning he came to a large tree. The wind was caught in its branches and called to him.

WI **Wind:** Oh, Medio Pollito, please help me! I am tangled up. Please get me free of these branches. 10

MP **Medio Pollito:** Help you? You can help yourself! I am off to Madrid to see the king! 11

Narrator: And Medio Pollito hopped and kicked down the road. Soon Medio Pollito came to the town. He saw the palace and began to hop up to the gate to wait for the king. The king's cook saw him.

C **Cook:** Aha! Here is just what I need. The king wants chicken broth with his dinner! 12

Narrator: The cook grabbed Medio Pollito and dropped him into a pot of water. Poor Medio Pollito felt very wet and cold.

MP **Medio Pollito:** Water, water! Please don't wet me! Have pity on me! 13

WA **Water:** Medio Pollito, if only you had helped me when I was choked with weeds. I am afraid I cannot help you now. 14

Narrator: Then the fire began to burn Medio Pollito.

MP **Medio Pollito:** Fire, fire! Please don't burn me. Have pity on me. 15

F **Fire:** Medio Pollito, if only you had helped me when I was dying. I am afraid I cannot help you now. 16

Narrator: Medio Pollito hurt so much that he thought he would die. Just then the cook lifted the lid of the pot.

C **Cook:** Oh, dear! This chicken is burned to a crisp. It is of no use to me. 17

Narrator: The cook threw Medio Pollito out the window. The wind blew him into the air.

MP **Medio Pollito:** Wind, wind. Please don't blow me along so fast. Have pity on me. 18

WI **Wind:** Medio Pollito, if only you had helped me when I was caught in the branches of the tree. I am afraid I cannot help you now. 19

Narrator: The wind blew Medio Pollito over the houses until they reached the highest church in town. It left him there on top of the steeple. That is where he stays. If you go to Madrid today and find the highest church, you will find Medio Pollito. He is perched on one leg with one wing and one ear. He doesn't hop and kick any more. He just looks out over the town with one sad eye.

PART 3

HENNY PENNY

 Narrator: One day Henny Penny was eating some corn in the farmyard. Smack! Something hit her on the head.

Henny Penny: Goodness! The sky is falling! I must go and tell the king. 1

Narrator: Henny Penny set off to see the king. Soon she met Cocky Locky.

Cocky Locky: Where are you going, Henny Penny? 2

Henny Penny: The sky is falling! I am going to tell the king! 3

Cocky Locky: May I come with you? 4

Henny Penny: Of course you may. 5

Narrator: So Henny Penny and Cocky Locky set off to tell the king that the sky was falling. Soon they met Ducky Lucky.

Ducky Lucky: Where are you going, Henny Penny and Cocky Locky? 6

Henny Penny and Cocky Locky: The sky is falling! We are going to tell the king! 7

Ducky Lucky: May I come with you? 8

Henny Penny and Cocky Locky: Of course you may. 9

Narrator: So Henny Penny, Cocky Locky, and Ducky Lucky set off to tell the king that the sky was falling. Soon they met Goosey Loosey.

Goosey Loosey: Where are you going, Henny Penny, Cocky Locky, and Ducky Lucky? 10

Henny Penny, Cocky Locky, and Ducky Lucky: The sky is falling! We are going to tell the king! 11

Goosey Loosey: May I come with you? 12

Henny Penny, Cocky Locky, and Ducky Lucky: Of course you may. 13

Narrator: So Henny Penny, Cocky Locky, Ducky Lucky, and Goosey Loosey set off to tell the king that the sky was falling. Soon they met Turkey Lurkey.

Turkey Lurkey: Where are you going, Henny Penny, Cocky Locky, Ducky Lucky, and Goosey Loosey? 14

Henny Penny, Cocky Locky, Ducky Lucky, and Goosey Loosey: The sky is falling! We are going to tell the king! 15

Turkey Lurkey: May I come with you?   16

Henny Penny, Cocky Locky, Ducky Lucky, and Goosey Loosey: Of course you may.   17

Narrator: So Henny Penny, Cocky Locky, Ducky Lucky, Goosey Loosey, and Turkey Lurkey set off to tell the king that the sky was falling. Soon they met Foxy Loxy.

Foxy Loxy: Where are you going, Henny Penny, Cocky Locky, Ducky Lucky, Goosey Loosey, and Turkey Lurkey?   18

Henny Penny, Cocky Locky, Ducky Lucky, Goosey Loosey, and Turkey Lurkey: The sky is falling! We are going to tell the king!   19

Foxy Loxy: But this is not the way to the king, Henny Penny, Cocky Locky, Ducky Lucky, Goosey Loosey, and Turkey Lurkey. I know the way. Shall I show you?   20

Henny Penny, Cocky Locky, Ducky Lucky, Goosey Loosey, and Turkey Lurkey: Yes! Please show us the way!   21

Narrator: So they all followed Foxy Loxy to tell the king that the sky was falling. Soon they came to the door of Foxy Loxy's cave.

Foxy Loxy: This is a shortcut to the king's. I will go first. You come after, Henny Penny, Cocky Locky, Ducky Lucky, Goosey Loosey, and Turkey Lurkey.   22

Henny Penny, Cocky Locky, Ducky Lucky, Goosey Loosey, and Turkey Lurkey: Of course!   23

Narrator: Turkey Lurkey was first into the cave. Foxy Loxy grabbed him and ate him up. Goosey Loosey was next. Foxy Loxy grabbed her and ate her, too. Ducky Lucky waddled into the cave next. Foxy Loxy grabbed him for his next meal. But when Cocky Locky came into the cave, Foxy Loxy was full and a bit slower. He grabbed for Cocky Locky, but missed. Cocky Locky ran out of the cave.

Cocky Locky: Henny Penny! Run home! The fox has eaten Turkey Lurkey, Goosey Loosey, and Ducky Lucky!   24

Narrator: So Cocky Locky and Henny Penny ran home. And the king never found out that the sky was falling.

ALPHABETICAL INDEX TO TALES

ABOUT THE AUTHOR

Suzanne I. Barchers received her bachelor of science degree in elementary education from Eastern Illinois University, her master's degree in education in reading from Oregon State University, and her doctor of education degree in curriculum and instruction from the University of Colorado, Boulder.

Ms. Barchers has been an educator and administrator for more than twenty years. She is a contributing author to *Learning* magazine and is the author of *Creating and Managing the Literate Classroom*; *Wise Women: Folk and Fairy Tales from Around the World*; and *Cooking Up U.S. History*.

Ms. Barchers is on the adjunct faculty at the University of Colorado, Denver, and is acquisitions editor for Teacher Ideas Press, a division of Libraries Unlimited. She continues to write in the area of language arts.